The Meaning of the Reading *between the lines*

The Meaning of the Reading *between the lines:*
The Esoteric Verse and Verve
of Edward V. Beck

authorHOUSE®

AuthorHouse™
1663 Liberty Drive
Bloomington, IN 47403
www.authorhouse.com
Phone: 1-800-839-8640

First published by AuthorHouse 01/12/2012

ISBN: 978-1-4685-3236-4 (sc)
ISBN: 978-1-4685-3235-7 (ebk)

Library of Congress Control Number: 2011963078

Printed in the United States of America

"The Preacher sought to find delightful words and to write words of truth correctly"

—Ecclesiastes 12:10

For Those Who Have Ears to Hear

"If a tree falls in the forest, and no one is around to hear it, does it make a sound?"—or so goes one of philosophy's staple questions. One might think the question too obvious, and reflexively cry, with careless impertinence: "but of course," wondering why so simple a question was posed. But even science will vouch that a receiver, a hearer, is needed for sound to be classified as sound. Thus, the compression of air that occurs within the ear canal that excites the many hair follicles that produces sound, when absent, begs this philosophical conundrum—this question about sound's existence. Of course, this riddle derives its intrigue from the fact that it is practically unresolvable: that it cannot be scientifically ascertained. And anything not scientifically determined does not exist in today's reality or within today's scientific imagination.

The smallest organism viewed through the lens of a microscope is larger than the largest stars; just as our myopic moon sometimes eclipses our sentient sun—and makes us walk by its secondary light—sometimes we see men as fuzzy trees in noiseless reveries. Beguiled by the madness of nearness and internally transported by the music of the distant spheres, implosions become louder than explosions and Black Holes more real than White Lights. When reality is measured only subjectively it ceases to be reality. Just as aloneness is unresolvable except by company and the noiseless felling of lone trees unnoticed except within the context of a large-scale deforestation project, so reality is only known in its entire subjective and objective context.

Yet the disconnection of disparate parts of reality, as splintering facets of knowledge, is behind all commonality of experience; it is illusory to think that artificiality—armless trunks banded together—can reach the status of natural limb and leaf and nature's intertwining embrace. Though the essential fiber of my own being is saturated with knowledge unknown to others, parsing me to the core will yield an essential fuel; whether I fall or remain erect is substantially a private affair, but the public eventually hears of my fall (and their scrutiny lights me on fire).

At the back of all there is to say is the lone voice, barely perceptible, even to a sophisticated or discerning ear. The clamor of the carpet and the tease of the trees are but the white noise canvas upon which the charred and black words accentuate their existence and meaning. Bold relief is needed to free one from the constraints of symmetry and indistinguishable existence. Beams and planks and boards are forms of a bygone glory and the skeletal frame upon which I now hang the weight of my internal world; outside lays my past experience among the groves of knotted oaks and lean majestic cedars. You heard that I was felled; you came and made the best of me. There upon the forest floor you came upon a silhouette of prostration, silent but for the creaking made lying across those ancient arms: my forbears embracing me and holding me out into the shafts of sunlight peaking through the hole in the now damaged canopy above. Like a Black Hole, I am known not for who or what I am (or was), but for space I now do not occupy. My legacy lingers and my past has a voice some have heard; but when I stood sentry over my solitude, when I boldly took my stand, no one saw or heard me.

Table of Contents

Working through it

"Does not the ear test words,
As the palate tastes its food?"

—Job 12:11

Dumb Drum

**"Who is this that darkens counsel
with words without knowledge?"—Job 38:1-2**

The wind will whistle, because words
are not in its vocabulary;
reason in not an article of speech
between its puckered lips; nary
does a rhythm heat,

when an argument is ensued
without the common sense;
it will carry away the unfounded
with its swift current essence
to the beat of a dumb drum.

At the Parting of the Sea Returning

An implosion of light!

Between the parted lips
Prophesying breaks out
Spilling the watery milk
Crying over the future
Confused direction
Escaping the darkness
Crossing the atmospheric line
Avoiding the left for dead
Ceasing broken waters

A child comes forth to stake his claim
Thrashing little steps everywhere and nowhere

There at the parting of the sea
Of humanity at its girth
Equitably split between polar worlds
Apart at the center of being
Torn between good and evil
A child rears itself as an apple
Of a mother's singular eye
From the narrow womb through pain
Center of attention getting
Baby constricting breath her conscience
Imparting the air of knowledge
Springing like oxidation from apple trees
To the still birthing short breathing child
A doctor administers his hand

There the drained mother lies
From the experience of extracting
The life of her son
From her broken watered womb

At the Parting of the Sea Returning
(cont...)

An implosion of being!

The child wishes he was never born
To have climatic experience
Crying about the issues and tissues
About his picked bones in union
Joined unanimously in joy
In the moving of mother's waters
Emotionally rippled and swelling
From the belly many tears
Yet to come and wash the eyes
And feet kicking the heels
At the displacing life

An implosion of darkness (disillusionment)!

A sad burdened mother without
A duct no longer to shed
The impassioned waters
Holy and deeply drowned
Considering her weakened
Failing heart of compassion
Stares beyond her powers
To comprehend the parting
Son dividing his ways
On the firm footed earth
That beneath his thinking
Supports his wandering
Flanking indiscriminate appetite
That heart burns his stomach
Of passions pursuing wild
Fatted calves to slaughter
And slake his sacrificial thirst
For the life blood
Of his own making wayward life

At the Parting of the Sea Returning

(cont...)

The imploded debris of light/being/darkness!

There, his still remains
To be seen placement in life
Between the parted sea
Sides stretched to the Promised Land
By the elastic interpretation of water
And its inclination to decline the world
Of its continued retaining
Wall of constricting room
To roam this claustrophobic world
A child opens wide his mouth to cry
And is drowned out by the moving
Returning sea.

A-Tributary

We, desiring an uninhibited flow
of form both liquid and solid
in matter and matters beyond
our capabilities seeking and probing
unexplored topics and topography
everywhere our heads dictating our feet
where we move unabashed and bashing
every party and funeral visiting
those gone and going inside
scurrying about like insects
squashing and treading wrath
grapes of our wine and whines
fueling the hollows of our thought patterns
breaking and static waving riding
to the shores and store windows
shopping and peeping through glasses
beyond mannequins into a sea
where the living swelling and cresting
souls' content is near finishing
populating the earth.

Habitual Brain Child

"Behold, I have found only this,
That God made men upright,
but they have sought out many devices"
—Ecclesiastes 7:29

The mind bemused with harrowment,
beside itself, with etched lines
drawn deeply into its brain,
like habits of foreboding import:
this, my conscience, needs assuagement.

Align the habits for absolution,
and color with penetrating oils,
this mind so devoid of artful dodging:
rutty, fretful, and personally
the subject of much consternation.

On Hell Fire

I burned my left arm on an iron
I had borrowed to press working clothes,
and like Job who cursed the day he was born,
I, unlike him, cursed what he would not.
Flashing quicker than the pain to my brain
(animal reflexion)
I mused as the fire raged within:
"Why am I ironing working clothes anyways?"
Could it be the scrutiny of appearance
of him who evaluates my every move
more closely than to my bosom
I'd play with fire?
I burned my left arm on an iron—
a most useless arm at that—
that for which it strives for mastery,
but to which the right is so much better.
I'd cast it aside if it were painless,
(just as I'm ordered to do)
but I have uses for uselessness;
besides, I couldn't handle the pain.

I Go a Certain Way

The path I took to schoolin'
Is tumbleweeded, brown, and blown;
Trampled more vigorously than wine,
But vacant as the vat drunk down,
I ambled and sometimes reeled
Like a pickled body on concrete.
Their intrepid gait and intimate shoes
Could not overcome the overwhelming hardness;
But where I've gone covers this ground
With multitudinous brown grass;
Still the untethered tumbleweed
Has taught my familiar feet to not walk
In both certitude and other people's shoes.

The path I took to schoolin'
Has been traversed before;
And the wind and grass, cut
Like clichés from a masterpiece,
Pronounce pedantic and trite sentences
Against the pedestrian and common good.
Nonetheless, I go a certain way.

Beneath the Raging Sea

She sits among waves of me calling:
whispers . . . but loud in appealing;
like a whirlpool, I succumb;
cascading, I completely come:
her woos, the substance, ripple my heart.

Splashes of guilt only add volume
as the water settles the spume.
So my heart lies at woo-man's feet;
she moors in me complete—
anchored in my flesh not to depart.

Wishy-washy I may seem to be;
volition that I make breaks down:
but there's a connection you don't see
where the floor of my ocean drowns.

Animism

My soul in latter days is thick
With animal viscosity;
It has solution, though sick
That oozes animosity;
"Be angry and sin not," it's said;
And consideration I've made
Of it—when in my human head.
But blood is riper than Hades
And fills my beast head with madness:
A raging fire of my badness.

Temper puts guilt in my blood;
But regardless of behavior
—Becoming an ape slinging mud
—This viscous red needs a savior.

My background
holds me in place

Like a butterfly pinned in a box
Openly displayed to opened eyes.

Enlightenment needs fuel to continue,
And my soul is on fire with thought:
Would that my soul was an endless source!
I'd imagine freedom as far as wingspan
Held open by wind and not the pins;
I'd fly as far as the fuel would give
Beyond the boundaries of my soul . . .

Oh I'd probably fall like Icarus did
Beyond the confines of the world's pull
Facing the sun in its blazing
Without a background to cast a shadow;

Against the cursed Earth I'd drop
From a distance no one could measure
'cept the God who'd know and deem me
A fanciful highfalutin fly
That sought the heights of Babel.

Me and My Shadows Know

Shadows no doubt are a part of me:
They form the boundaries I encompass;
They reach dismemberingly across the bridges,
Those broken bridges I've left behind;
They overtake ground I only consider;
Everywhere I go, they lead or follow;
Everywhere I have vision, they know;
No doubt, my shadows understand;
You see, they've been in my closets
And picked the bones with me.

There are no secrets to discover,
No light to obscure with my form,
That my shadows haven't contended with,
That they haven't absorbed,
Assimilated,
And made their own.

Shall I dung the little tree?

Shall I dung the little tree
(unbridled, sap-full)
that bends and curtsies
almost politely, giddy
against the winded breath
(old yet amorous)
of a storm raging among a still
fertile grove
and a narrow-banded trunk,
straight, upright,
however constrained,
even in this foremost gale?

Shall I overshadow her world
with my expansive one,
stooping to meet her hungry eyes,
and winking at the tender shoots
sprouting, spouting
childlike fairy tales
to woo her fancy?

Or shall I take to her
the mature and dark shade,
the underlying intent,
the overlaid eunuch-barked branches
above her little tree top
unsuspecting?

Just Beneath the Clouds

There is sunshine beyond the clouds
Way above our puny heads
Beyond the secondary light of moonshine
And her third cousin's twinkling
Stars that brighten the show;
Beyond the production of our collective heads
Beyond the ramifications of our conceived
Conceited eternal destinies
Beyond the mechanical eyes' reach
Light has yet to illuminate
Our mortal souls.

Satellites circle our circumferences
And answer every angle we inspire,
But when
Oh when!
You mortal souls
Will you understand
Just
And only just
What is clouded?

The Boastful Pride of Life

"For all that is in the world, the lust of the flesh
and the lust of the eyes
and **the boastful pride of life**, is not from the Father,
but is from the world"
(1 John 2:16, emphasis mine, NASB).

To my true colors pledge I allegiance
With an uplifted strong hand
To myself opened in the wind
A cape against the sky
Superimposed against the heavens
Above and beneath my expansive
Fraying extent of my full blown soul
Unfurled and snapping raging glory
I to the contemptible wind cast myself
From the top of a tall building
Leapt from a single bound bolt of fabric
The essence of my strength
To the view of all mortal needs
My lion my heart flapping
Spent at the inflamed skies extinguishing
Light at the end of the day
Sliding down the pole
And folding myself into night
Abating the inner turmoil of swirling fire
That ignites in me again tomorrow

My Dad's Gray is not Hereditary

I am color blind and not too diplomatic;
rather long-sighted, narrow and black
(the artistic eye in me is obscure and back)
I see so well in white and black.

Be vague, and I'll lose the light of day
in the foggy fringe-mind attractions
of amoral doting and moral gray.
I'm sorry—I abhor shadowy abstractions!

"Between black and white is grayness,
and not all is sufficiently defined;"
or so are the workings of his greatness
(we must compromise some—that's fine)
but to shadeless truth I must bind.

Sonnets

"A wise man will hear and increase in learning,
And a man of understanding will acquire wise counsel,
To understand a proverb and a figure,
The words of the wise and their riddles."

—Proverbs 1:5-6

Common Ground

The soul is as fragile as a flower
Blooming noble amidst peon grasses.
You can see its regal head above classes
First to receive the crowning sun's power.
But the light of day is no deterrent
To the soul that knows not the common plight.
Shade that's cast is cast greater than the night
In the kingdom of flowers resurgent!
For as one soul is laid in dust, so two
Rises to replace the essence of one!
And all the flowers in all the kingdom
Cannot the surface cover with its hue;
Beneath the fleshly blades is life begun,
The flowers of kings and all of serfdom.

The Simple Christian

Who is as blind as the one God sends?
He has no agenda, no opinion;
He's not ambitious, has no dominion;
Like an animal that cannot pretend,
A loner that follows no popular trend,
This, the man of God, the simple Christian,
Comes to you in varied loss of vision:
Light from darkness is hard to comprehend!

Forgive him, for he knows not what he does;
He hardly knows who he is, or who he was;
But it is truer in retrospection,
(Even further so upon reflection),
Within his spirit enlightenment flares,
Consuming inner darkness that impairs.

Basking in the
Lesser Light of Recall

But for the god dying inside of me,
That scant slant of light bent over backwards
Inside my gut, I'd welcome afterwards
Certain understanding of memory.
But I've not immortal capacity:
Not the seer's eyes, nor the prophet's words;
No comprehension backwards or forwards.
My refracted soul will have ceased to be

When the moon forgets to reflect the sun.
Since I cannot foresee this being done,
I'd be smart to remember yesterdays:
Those clear and straight as the arrow flies ways,
When I knew without a shadow of doubt,
The sun did shine and the moon did about.

Honeysuckle winds move the weathervane

Honeysuckle winds move the weathervane,
And so too my heart when I inhale her
Odorless perfume and wake-less demure
Gliding across a liquid windowpane.
Her ghost cannot long linger in this rain
As my heart can't miss a beat and be pure;
Hope is a molten mirror, to be sure:
Elastic as inner vision is vain.

My heart is but a sculpture made of ice
And frozen fire: a monumental price
Of desire unrealized; a phantom hold
On my soul: disillusion to unfold.
O' that she were to materialize
Conjuring up her form before my eyes!

In the Twinkling Apple of an Eye

There's nothing more beautiful than she
Upon whom my eyes cannot look away;
Eyes of mortal flesh to this weakness sway!
Call it lust, call it power; but I'll be
No deeper than skin which overwhelms me.
It is not a choice, nor desire, per se:
It is the essence of flesh without may.
Maybe I'll restrain myself just to see

If the insistent urge to sin should go;
Maybe I'll put blinders on and walk straight.
But there's nothing I've seen that I don't know!
These eyes are flesh and they participate.
But Christ has rent the veil and forever
Made beauty something more than Eve or her.

Pity me Edna
St. Vincent Millay

Pity me Edna St. Vincent Millay
For my stronger vessel anatomy;
Pity me that I should be cursed this way,
Bearing all the responsibility!
Pity me for having pitied your kind:
For opening doors and my heart's desire;
For seeing you clearer in my swift mind
Than my slow masculine heart can inspire.

This I have known always: love is stronger
"Than the wide blossom which the wind assails;"
But I've not understood who was the wronger
In the past loves that came to no avails.
I just know the maleness of my own heart
Better than a woman spilling her art.

The Forbidden Fruit

Vacant is the shallow socket where lies
The panes of gray glassy undistinguished
Portals where runs the saint and extinguished
Soul into the Catacomb of the mind's eyes.
There, in the recessed inner man, like sties
That swine would seek as a muddy home squished
Beneath their cloven hoofs, we relinquished
Our vision through rivers of soulish cries.

O' that the sweat could but dry for awhile!
That the tears of hardened flesh could produce
Unimpeded fruit, instead of this guile!
Then would I save my skin, and introduce
The sanctity of imagination;
Then I'd live without investigation!

Spiritual Organ Donation

They say that gods have mouths to inspire me;
Or at least, I can by myself surmise
That to convey their intent they need eyes,
Or something still like a nose, hand, or knee
To bounce me upon in the wind with glee—
Little child tossed to and fro in the skies
Past deciding intentions, signs, or whys—
These are the gods' inspiration to me.

So I'll write frolicking lines with my blood,
And possess my vessel in their honor;
I'll scribble like madness and sling the mud
To tell everyone that I'm a donor!
But to you, O' Recipient, go now
In this your new strength—and don't question how.

Revelation Fire

Before the caveman knew the useful fire,
Before the little boy played with matches,
Before stars had fallen through the hatches
Of heaven's covering cherubim, the pyre
Awaited angels' wind to inspire
Man. But strange fire, doors without latches,
Do freely upon mans' inner thatches
Burn too deep, and razes proper desire.

Let your bush be ablaze with God's glory,
Your heart with unmolested history.
Pages turn in wind, but not all is of God;
Fate is not whimsical, sure or slipshod:
In His light we see light, and understand;
If not, heat shall be added to light and . . .

The Cannibalization
of Our Purpose

Eating one's heart out

The spirit of man is simply a hole
Where God peeps inside and we back at him:
Our baffled demeanor filled to the brim,
Compartmentalizing the human soul,
Pressed against our transparent and mere role,
There at the outer limits of a whim,
We, from our center, go out on a limb
And fail to secure the essential goal.

When the scrutiny of God withers our core
We've misinterpreted his kind intent:
Retracting into wormholes, we escape
Into the meat we must now devour
If we are ever to simply relent
From our insistent and self-imposed rape

There's a Yellow Bird

There's a yellow bird frozen in my head
That I once saw lifeless on a window
Laid horizontal. I could not see though,
And it escapes me 'bout this scene once dead,
Now alive from something somebody said:
"Close the skylight to keep those birds out!" No
Amount of sun and glass can ever throw
Enough magnification on what's dread!

The pale sun flickers and can't thaw the ice
Coated yellow bird. Bygone paradise
Cannot my imagination inspire.
I, doomed to die, die and die the higher
The more I dream and make my hope to fly,
Cowardice begets wings and lights the sky.

Upon Dylan's *Fern Hill*

Now as I was young and lilting as Thomas
Green and lit upon the steep jaded hills
Of ferns and grasses overgrowing thrills
I became King of mountains of promise
I grew strong and fortified my power
I shored up the waving thoughts in my head
Drowned dissenters in my watershed
And shut my kingdom's gates in the wee hour

And there in solitary confinement
I rehashed Dylan's words of refinement
Oh that I were green like grass and not jade!
That I could break the chains I have made!
If I should be overturned in my head
Be it known that I'd rather die instead

When science
is the only god you see

Upon my baring soul, who would dare say
To God Almighty without restraint: "why?"
And have the gumption of peerless Job's eye
To see all encompassingly the day
That before the sun should rise tomorrow,
The end of all matter in the Big Bang?
But if you understand, may your head hang
Which curses God and brings down one sparrow.
Without a quaking from faith and conscience
Your premise on this shaky earth shatters
Under the microscope of scrutiny.
Where is the undoing of the pretense
And the discovering of what matters
When science is the only God you see?

Wormhole Salvation

Implosions are just explosions expressed
Another way, as Black Holes are notions
That explain unexplainable motions
Of heavenly bodies as they are pressed
Beyond the limits of known law. Compressed
Substance—now more substantial; Emotions—
Now more heart-felt. Religious devotions
Condensing import like feelings regressed.

The pressure inside is a perversion
Of makeup, just as death is inversion
Of life somewhere else. Weakness bulges where
The essence gathers and compels our prayer.
Through the eye of a needle we go home,
Bare as a baby, skinny as a poem.

Epiphanous
Musings

"The words of a man's mouth are deep waters;
The fountain of wisdom is a bubbling brook."

—Proverbs 18:4

The Glandular Boys

My reflection upon hearing one too many news reports
about some manchild behaving like a seasoned adult criminal.

A sperm of truth has not reached these eggs
These hated fated mated eggs:
The scourge of every glandular boy
That would a man be
Except a condition
Of being a rendition of the human soul:
A product of a byproduct of an afterbirth.

Never held or loved
But mostly
Never told the truth
These glandular boys are muscular men
Able to swing most productively
From limb to overhanging limb
Never touching the ground.

So the glandular boys hang like men
From a tree
Out on a limb
Overhanging
Overextended
Over.

Splitting Personality Hairs

The extremities,
Hanging long in sockets
Stretched to the limits of reason,
Intuitively know
How to act and react
To the various stimulations
Of living tissue.
Sharp points felt and interpreted
By both hands, inflexibly
Holding their respective
Positions of perspective:
Strong opinions held
Open and outstretched.

Strong hands grasp
The weight of their view
In a lean and athletic posture
Extended at arm's length
In a prolonged protracted
Reaching for strict meaning.

Splitting Personality Hairs

(cont...)

The extremities,
Hanging long in sockets
Stretched to the limits of reason
Physically know
How to act and react
To the internal shocks
Of divided nerve
Endings at the extent
Of the appropriate
Grasped objective
(subjective to the full reach
Of the brain).

Holding firm
Their respective weights
Of responsibility,
Each hand, armed
With a particular grasp,
Tire from their prolonged protracted
Reaching for true meaning.
Slowly these singular weights drop
Their respective prejudicial arms
(Their unnatural long held positions)
Leaving them now dangling
Like hair from heads
With split ends
At both ends.

Revelation Knowledge

My poring soul did nothing find
Seeking knowledge and godly kind.
Much wisdom makes my conscience sore
–Pouring soul to God brings me more.
"Knowledge is good," so I hit books:
Soothe my soul and please my high looks.
O' that knowledge could raise the dead!
–I'd read my soul from morn to bed;
But on my knees and while asleep
I gain vision my soul to keep.
So gather my head!—but it's been said:
–Nothing new—but in breaking bread.

Durst

if the twinkle in my eye
has leapt the space of us
and formed in your opinion:
then what am I to do
'cept to do the daring I do?

Fair-Weathered Friends

The bough unbroken
Holding myriad
Bright tongues unspoken,

(Promises that had
Been kept all season,
Now displayed like mad
Pigment of treason),
Say your peace and go!

There is no reason
To waggle or show
Your extended limb,
Your soul, what you know,

And those leaves in trim.
It's apparent now!
We've seen to the brim

All there is and how,
Summer and the bough.

Wishbone

I should have been patient
Through those drying days;
More frugal in removing all flesh.
But I unwisely heeded your pull
And played the wishbone game.

Maybe you coerced my hand
(But I held my end tightly)
And you pulled the larger part.
I can't say you cheated,
But I feel cheated nonetheless.

If I had known what was at stake
(and how colossally you'd divine me)
I never would have allowed you
Such immediate access to my heart.

Subconscious

In the shadow you make
I hide
and seek the answer to your
questions
How thoughtfully
you ponder and pose

and   skip

on purpose beyond me
The substance is with you
with me
there is darkness
Should you look
my way
you'd no doubt
miss me
I'd have to turn with you
and by reason of
your action
you'd never know me
but
like the shadow
you cast
I'm cast
in all your
story

Twilight

Where the days go spent
I wish they'd alone
Descend their descent,

Passing and bemoaned,
As shadows in Fall,
The mark that's my own!

It's here that I stall
To understand this:
Twilight is but pall,

Foreshadowing mist;
The dark in darkness,
The substance of gist;

The like in likeness,
An eclipsing moon;
Something in Loch Ness,

And the night too soon:
Pessimistic noon!

The Specific Gravity of Humanism

There is a specific gravity:
the weight of individuality
measured against, unilaterally,
all the sea of humanity.
A drop-in-the-bucket mentality
has the one who sees clearly
nothing of apparent reality,
but values his responsibility
above the high tide of unity.
Humanism, in its simplicity,
ignores inherent complexity,
and would take men out contextually
from his person he uses habitually,
and would fill his drop-mentality
with oceans of unified integrity!
Is it that we must circumspectly
walk within a world gravity,
whose weight we feel universally,
that imposes this quandary?
We answer from obscurity:
in the thinking light of creativity,
with the mind of our nativity,
in a way that seems rightly,
we conclude our human divinity.

New under the sun—man's divinity!
"Ye are gods –but will die like men," blasphemy.
In this New Age, there is, distinctively,
a complex and brilliant disparity,
against one Whole Man in His dignity
Who walked beneath His majesty!

Maybe the Means
Justify the End?

Halls to rooms unlit by my hand
are not easy to negotiate;
the halls are not my doing:
to light them, I hesitate.

I stay in my room all day
(except to traverse to another).
What need is there of hall light
when seldom do I pass there?

But halls are the connection
which tie my world together:
so I'll light the blessed halls,
and see if life gets better!

Once Upon a Time

Once upon a time
I timed a once
Far far away
Within my forest mind.
At arm's length
I went a-wandering
To seek a patch of heaven
Amongst my cloistered wood.

But fairy tales are only true
In fairy tales
And time is only true once
Except in perfect memory.

The Foolishness of Preaching
(without a sermon)

There beneath the vastness
An expansive knowledge
From the cuff from his fist
Of rage clenched brain
Sucker-punching the meek sky
Rippling vascular neck
Pumping up a highway of blood
With volume on high
From a strong presumptuous heart
A fool screams his Pointed Pointless Points

Over there beside his vastness
There at the distilling of everything
Uninhibited by mortal
Second guesses and comings
The large man drunk with himself
Makes small talk
Loud and unassuming
(Assuming of course
There's a point to preaching
Without a sermon)

The Way

"he that believeth shall not make haste . . ."
—Isaiah 28:16, partial.

Speed is a thrill to those
who need a course to overlay;
not with the quickness imposed,
but the question posed:
"To what do I owe this day?"

Another way has only confused;
a slower pace seemingly refused
timing and this query fused.
Stop-watch the entire race!—no
course discernable is mused.

Speed is a thrill to those
who need an answer still:
they want the course they chose!
They've hastily overlaid their toes
upon the race only patience will.

It seems to me

that an active mind
cannot conclude
in this lifetime
all the matters at hand,
at least;
and should not consider
beyond the scope
of the natural eye,
at most;
but most of all,
it seems to me,
conclusively,
that more than mind
was brought to bear
to understand
this.

He placed Eternity in our Hearts

"Like apples of gold in settings of silver
Is a word spoken in right circumstances."

—Proverbs 25:11

He placed eternity in our hearts

"He has made everything appropriate in its time.
He has also set eternity in their heart,
yet so that man will not find out the work which
God has done from the beginning even to the end"
—Ecclesiastes 3:11

In the meeting of the spending of time and its rending
of reality in full measure, brimmed with the moment,
I feel and think a treasure throughout my
comportment:
for the time is now ending that within was lending
and must move ahead where meant.

Yonder Ponder

When the tide is high and lit
by the moon in a cloudless night;
when atmosphere breathes light,
and the flaring scent sees fit
to overwhelm this man with fright;

when all the world beneath the sea
is swollen covered in a wake;
when each star is wished and spake:
where then shall I be?

Beauty for Ashes

When upon my knees
I came to be
Smitten by stone
Symphonies

I arose to Thee
With more than me
Kissed by my own
Sympathies

Across A Cross

I've seen the dead and their dying,
I've witnessed the passing in the past;
I've known the soul that lived trying;
In all, the soul endeavored to last.

Across the tilted sphere a-spinnin'
It wobbled as it worked and played.
I've seen the troubled good it's been in
And the good trouble from which it prayed.

It moved across the land and sea—
Across the whitened heads a-sway—
It waited patiently to be
A soul ready for the Lord's Day.

Across a cross to the other side,
Beyond the horizon of a forever sky,
Past the grasp of Satan's pride,
A passing soul makes sweet bye and bye.

Understanding the Matter

In that hour Jesus rejoiced in spirit, and said,
I thank thee, O Father, Lord of heaven and earth,
that thou hast hid these things from the wise and prudent,
and hast revealed them unto babes: even so, Father;
for so it seemed good in thy sight"—Luke 10:21.

The pall like drapes hides the light
except a glimmer vertically shown
hung over the window of souls
where the highest revelation
twinkles in the vast blinking eye.
A Big Bang is not heard,
nor brilliance comprehended:
this light blinds minds' eyes
where the matter propels us yet.
Reverberations are heartfelt
and understood by children.
Behind the rented veil
creation is reconfigured;
and when all the dust has settled,
and all the matter disseminated,
existence will be understood
even by the aged and wise.

Be It Small

A house divided is not a rarity
And the sand upon which it stands
Will not subdue the house immediately
There is time, be it small, to understand

Call it grace or the brace of youth
But a pondering heart and head with couth
Has the time to search and occupy man
There is space, be it small, to understand

There are footprints in the sand for sure
Not prints of children but the mature
Wisdom is justified of her children for all
There is time, there is space, be it small

The Titantic and The Nautile:

*Upon reading an article about Jennifer Carter, who, on August 9, 1987,
became the first woman to dive down to the Titantic wreckage lying
12,500 feet below the sea in a bright yellow submersible named Nautile.*

Unsinkable man-made as can be
Is this Titantic and Frozen century
"amid the wreckage of human pride;"
Bedecked more than sufficient,
Run by earthly ore,
And sunk in a cold state of a colder sinker:
Who prescribed this maiden descent?
"they never slowed down
As they entered a field of icebergs . . ."

What awesome Man of foresight,
This one-hundred-and-fifty-nine-light-Man,
Who should lose confidence
In this unearthly sinking plight?

So stark "the wreckage" is, where
The Nautile came to see;
But she, so easily,
Arose on milled strand and prayer.

In Memoriam

to Clara Rae:

I saw you once so long ago
And I cherish to my surprise
The smallness of the snow
And smaller still my eyes

That I should see you there
Is nothing short of strange
Where time cannot impair
Nor essence rearrange

Before my father's gleam
Before the snow had steeped
I saw you in my dream
And before my years I reaped

I saw you once so long ago
From a picture that I hold
Snow melts and my eyes go
But you never grow old

Ode to a Black Swan

(Aka M. Antoinette)

She has a beauty all her own
Convention she beguiles
Beneath the world she is known
Like a mirror is to smiles

There upon the glass she glides
And in her wake a promise
Subtle as the sun it hides
Astride a doubting Thomas

Disilluding light is sure
The Land of Enchantment is
To think only white is pure
Is to narrow where she is

She has a beauty all her own
Convention she beguiles
Beneath the world she is known
Like a mirror is to smiles

The Final Word

"Because in much wisdom there is much grief,
and increasing knowledge results in increasing pain."
—Ecclesiastes 1:18

I sought to grasp the meaning
Yet failed to understand;
So I labored for gleaning
But measured reprimand.

Suddenly He grasped me with His hand
(And I came to realize)
The abundance of the land
And the apple of His eyes:

By the power of observation
All I see is sorrow;
But by the word of revelation,
There's a tomorrow.